Living Fossils

Clues to the Past

Caroline Arnold • *Illustrated by* Andrew Plant

For Paige, Lucas, and Alessandra—C. A.

To science teachers—guiding lights in a confusing world—A. P.

Special thanks to Carl Mehling at the American Museum of Natural History for his expertise.

Published by Charlesbridge
85 Main Street, Watertown, MA 02472
(617) 926-0329 • www.charlesbridge.com

Illustrations done in acrylic paint on acid-free art paper
Display type set in Block Berthold by Adobe
Text type set in Today by Veronika Elsner
Color separations by Colourscan Print Co Pte Ltd, Singapore
Printed by Imago in China
Production supervision by Brian G. Walker
Designed by Whitney Leader-Picone

Library of Congress Cataloging-in-Publication Data
Arnold, Caroline, author.
    Living fossils: clues to the past/Caroline Arnold;
Illustrated by Andrew Plant.
        pages cm
    ISBN 978-1-58089-691-7 (reinforced for library use)
    ISBN 978-1-60734-836-8 (ebook)
    ISBN 978-1-60734-837-5 (ebook pdf)
1. Living fossils—Juvenile literature. 2. Animals, Fossil—Juvenile
literature. I. Plant, Andrew, illustrator. II. Title.

QL88.5.A76 2015
591—dc23   2014049180

Printed in China
(hc) 10 9 8 7 6 5 4 3 2 1

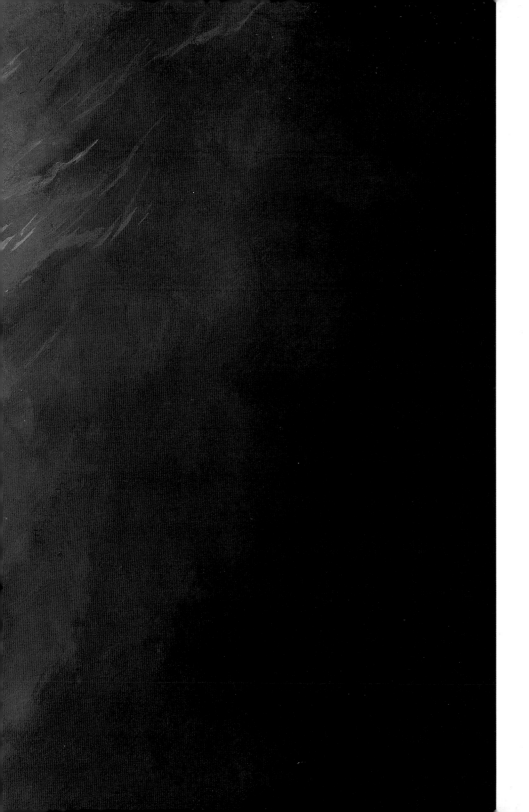

An Ancient Survivor, the Coelacanth

In December 1938, fishermen off the east coast of South Africa pulled up a strange-looking fish. It was five feet long and pale blue, with an unusually large, lobed tail. The fishermen gave the fish to Marjorie Courtenay-Latimer, the curator of a local museum. She had never seen anything like it, so she sent a sketch to Professor J. L. B. Smith, a fish expert. When he saw the drawing, he was astounded. It looked almost exactly like the coelacanth, a fish thought to have died out about sixty-five million years earlier. How could this fish, missing from the fossil record for tens of millions of years, still be swimming in the ocean? Why had it survived when so many other species had become extinct? What could it reveal about life in prehistoric times? The fish appeared to be a "living fossil."

about 385 million years ago

about 70 million years ago

4

today

Snapshots in Time

A living fossil is an informal term for a modern-day plant or animal that closely resembles its ancient relatives. It often has no close living relatives. The term "living fossil" was first used in 1859 by British scientist Charles Darwin in his book *On the Origin of Species*. He used it when discussing the platypus, an animal that retains features of some of the earliest mammals.

Most living things change as the world around them changes. They adapt to new conditions. Usually changes happen slowly. Fossils provide a record of these changes. They are snapshots of moments in time going back millions of years. They show us that living things have evolved into new forms and become new species. Living fossils are a mystery: Why did they change so little when the world around them changed so much? Why didn't they become extinct?

A fossil is any part of a plant or animal that is preserved in some way. Fossils can show us the size and shape of ancient plants and animals. They can also tell us where plants and animals lived and what other living things shared the environment. But fossils show us less about how animals moved, communicated, and interacted, or how plants smelled or what color they were.

Living fossils are a link between the prehistoric world and the present. We know where these plants and animals live today, what they need to grow, how they reproduce, and other details of their lives. This helps us figure out what helped them survive. Because living fossils are so similar in appearance to their ancestors, it is likely that they live and behave in much the same way as their ancestors did.

fossil of a coelacanth

Horseshoe Crabs Then

One hundred fifty million years ago, a horseshoe crab crawled onto the shore of a shallow lagoon in what is now southern Germany and searched for worms and shellfish in the damp sand. Nearby, dinosaurs preyed on insects and small animals, and lizards sat in the sun. In the air, winged reptiles soared and one of the earliest birds, *Archaeopteryx*, flapped its wings. The horseshoe crab returned to the water and later died. Sediment slowly covered the horseshoe crab's body. Over time the lagoon dried up and the seabed hardened to limestone, preserving the buried animal as a fossil.

Trails in the sand made by a horseshoe crab's long tail, or telson, have been preserved as fossils.

9

Horseshoe Crabs NOW

On a warm summer night, a full moon shines over a sandy beach on the east coast of the United States. Hundreds of horseshoe crabs emerge from the water. The female crabs pull themselves up the beach, dragging the males, which hold onto their backs. Each female digs a hole and deposits a cluster of tiny eggs. The males fertilize the eggs, and the crabs return to the sea. Waves wash sand into the nest, covering the eggs. A few weeks later the eggs hatch and thousands of tiny horseshoe crabs scuttle to the water. As they grow, they search for worms and shellfish to eat. One day some will return to this same shore to lay their own eggs, just as horseshoe crabs have likely done for millions of years.

HOW THEY SURVIVE

- Horseshoe crabs have hard shells that completely cover their small bodies and protect them from predators.

- They can live in water with a wide range of temperatures and salt levels.

- They are able to go for months with little or no food.

Dragonflies Then

An early relative of the dragonfly, the size of a crow, chased smaller insects across what is now the Kansas prairie. Back then, 280 million years ago, eastern Kansas was a coastal plain dotted with small lakes and marshes. The warm, moist air buzzed with hundreds of insects, including ancestors of today's dragonflies, mayflies, earwigs, grasshoppers, and cicadas. Sometimes insects fell into the water, sank, and became covered in mud. As the lakes and marshes dried up, the buried insects became fossils.

A fossil of the dragonfly relative Meganeuropsis *was found near Elmo, Kansas. It had a wingspan of twenty-eight inches and is the largest insect ever known.*

Dragonflies NOW

On a warm summer day, dragonflies dart after flies and mosquitoes over a Kansas pond. Their colorful bodies and iridescent wings flash in the sun. Dragonflies can move their wings independently, allowing them to fly forward, backward, up, or down, like miniature helicopters. Below the pond's surface, young dragonflies, called nymphs, catch small aquatic insects and other food. Nymphs live entirely in the water. As their bodies grow, they molt, shedding their outer covering. A nymph may molt up to fifteen times. On its last molt the nymph emerges from the water, grows wings, and becomes an adult. Then it takes off into the air, ready to hunt and look for a mate.

HOW THEY SURVIVE

- Dragonflies are extremely agile fliers and can reach top speeds of 30 miles per hour or more, which helps them catch prey and avoid birds, frogs, and other predators.

- Dragonflies have keen eyesight, good for spotting and following prey.

- Large mandibles in their mouths chew prey quickly, making it easy for dragonflies to eat on the move.

Sphenodontids Then

Dinosaurs walked and winged reptiles flew 180 million years ago in a canyon in what is now northeastern Mexico. Small lizard-like reptiles called sphenodontids darted among the ferns and horsetails, catching insects in their wide jaws. Meanwhile, on the mountain above the canyon, a volcano rumbled and spewed smoke into the air. Suddenly the volcano erupted. Falling ash rained down into the canyon, trapping and burying the animals that lived there. Over time their bones became fossils.

With two rows of upper teeth and one row of lower teeth, sphenodontids easily crushed their prey.

Sphenodontids NOW

As darkness falls on a rocky island off the coast of New Zealand, a tuatara emerges from its burrow. It is ready for a night of hunting. Good eyesight helps it spot its prey. This reptile also has a third eye on the top of its head, hidden by a layer of scales. The extra eye can sense light and may help the tuatara detect the time of day or season of the year.

Tuataras are a kind of sphenodontid. They are the only members of the group that are not extinct. Millions of tuataras once lived on the two main islands of New Zealand. When humans arrived about eight hundred years ago, they brought rats and dogs, and later, cats and ferrets. Tuatara eggs and hatchlings were easy prey for these predators, and the population on the two main islands was soon wiped out. Tuataras are now found on only a few small islands off the New Zealand coast. They are an endangered species.

HOW THEY SURVIVE

- When a tuatara is caught by a predator, its tail can break off, allowing it to escape.
- A tuatara's bodily processes are slow. It can go an hour without breathing if necessary.
- Unlike most other reptiles, tuataras remain active in cool weather.
- Their island homes have isolated tuataras from most predators.

Chambered Nautiloids Then

Seventy million years ago a warm, shallow sea covered the middle of North America, stretching from the Arctic to the Gulf of Mexico. Giant clams lived on the muddy bottom. Flightless birds paddled on the surface and dove after fish. Graceful chambered nautiloids propelled themselves through the water alongside their larger relatives, the ammonites. Nautiloids and ammonites had to watch for giant sea reptiles called mosasaurs. A mosasaur's sharp teeth could pierce a nautiloid's hard spiral shell to get at its soft body. Sometimes when a nautiloid or ammonite died, its empty shell sank to the sea bottom and became a fossil.

Visible bite marks on fossils of nautiloids and ammonites show that they were preyed upon by large sea reptiles.

Chambered Nautiloids NOW

In the deep, cool water off Australia's Great Barrier Reef, a chambered nautilus rests by day. At night this modern-day relative of ancient chambered nautiloids rises to shallower depths to hunt for food. Like a jet-propelled flying saucer, it swims after shrimp, crabs, and fish. The nautilus grabs its prey with long tentacles, pulls it into its beak-like mouth, and crushes it.

Like their ancient relatives, today's nautiluses must avoid ocean predators. When an octopus, shark, or turtle approaches, the nautilus retreats into its hard shell and closes the entrance with a tough, leathery hood.

HOW THEY SURVIVE

- Protective coloring helps a nautilus avoid predators. Seen from above, its stripes blend into the dark ocean. From below, its white shell blends into the sky.

- A nautilus can tolerate extreme changes in temperature and pressure, allowing it to live in a variety of habitats. It is found at a range of depths, from 300 feet below the ocean surface to the dark, cold water 2,000 feet below.

- It needs to eat only once every two weeks or less.

Latonia Frogs Then

In a mountain valley in central Italy a million and a half years ago, there was a large lake where turtles swam, ducks built nests, and deer, bears, and mammoths came to drink. Large frogs called *Latonia* hopped through the dense underbrush of the surrounding swamp as they searched for insects. Over time the climate changed. The animals in this warm, lush valley died, and the lake and swamps dried up. The dead plants piled up and compressed into peat, which then compacted and formed into coal. Mixed with the coal were the fossil remains of plants and animals, including many *Latonia* fossils.

Quarries at Pietrafitta in central Italy (near Perugia) contain thousands of Latonia *fossils.*

Latonia Frogs NOW

In 2011 a ranger at a nature preserve in the Hula Valley in northern Israel spotted an unusual frog with a bumpy back and a white-speckled belly. It was a rare Hula painted frog. Only a few of these frogs had ever been found, and none had been seen since the 1950s, when the large lake and swamps in the Hula Valley had been drained. But somehow a few frogs must have survived—mating, laying eggs, and producing more frogs. By 2013, thirteen more Hula painted frogs were discovered.

When the Hula painted frog was first identified in 1940, it was classified with other painted frogs. However, recent genetic testing shows that the Hula painted frog is actually a part of *Latonia*, a group that scientists thought had died out about fifteen thousand years ago. As the only living representative of *Latonia*, the Hula painted frog offers the chance to learn about its ancient relatives. It is a living fossil.

WILL THEY SURVIVE?

- Hula painted frogs are found only in the Hula Valley in a small area set aside as a nature preserve.

- The dense undergrowth around the marshes where the frogs live makes them hard to find and provides some protection from birds and other predators.

- The Hula painted frog population is so small and the habitat so limited that they are extremely endangered.

Clues to the Past

Many scientists are uncomfortable with the term "living fossil" because it suggests that the plants and animals did not evolve or change. They did. Either at a genetic level or through subtle physical changes, their bodies are different from those of their ancient relatives. Nevertheless they share many features in their outward appearance. Because of these similarities the plants and animals that we call living fossils can help us imagine their ancestors' lives long ago. Whether living fossils survived because they were isolated, hardy, able to live in a variety of conditions, or lacked competition, they are clues to the past. They make the prehistoric world come alive.

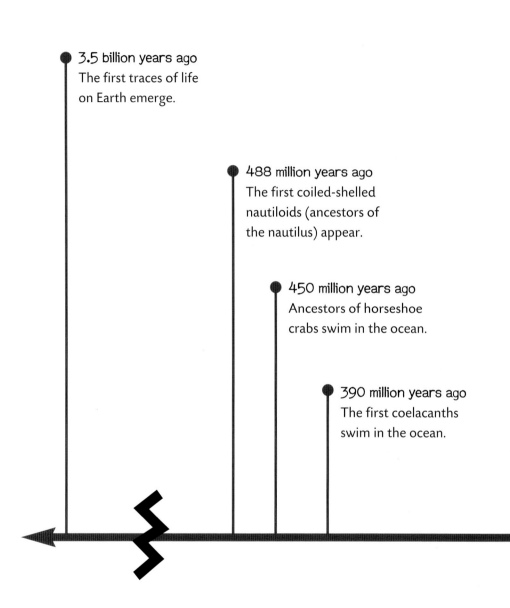

3.5 billion years ago
The first traces of life on Earth emerge.

488 million years ago
The first coiled-shelled nautiloids (ancestors of the nautilus) appear.

450 million years ago
Ancestors of horseshoe crabs swim in the ocean.

390 million years ago
The first coelacanths swim in the ocean.

325 million years ago
The first dragonfly relatives appear.

250 million years ago
Dragonfly relatives become extinct. The first true dragonflies appear.

225 million years ago
The first sphenodontids (small, lizard-like reptiles) appear.

65 million years ago
The Mesozoic era (the dinosaur age) ends. Coelacanths disappear from the fossil record and seem to be extinct.

60 million years ago
Sphenodontids die out—except for the tuatara.

23 million years ago
The first *Latonia* appear.

15,000 years ago
Latonia disappear from the fossil record and seem to be extinct.

1859 CE
Darwin publishes *On the Origin of Species* and coins the term "living fossil."

1938 CE
A coelacanth is discovered in waters off the coast of South Africa.

1940 CE
A Hula painted frog is found in what is now Israel.

2013 CE
Genetic testing shows that Hula painted frogs are in the *Latonia* genus and are living fossils.

Living Fossils

Coelacanth *(Latimeria chalumnae)*

After seeing the preserved skin of the strange fish found by Marjorie Courtenay-Latimer, Professor J. L. B. Smith confirmed its identification as a coelacanth and published a scientific paper announcing its discovery. (To honor Marjorie Courtenay-Latimer, the scientific name of the coelacanth, *Latimeria chalumnae*, includes part of her name.) Professor Smith then searched for more coelacanth specimens, but had to wait fourteen years before another one was caught. Coelacanths have since been found near the Comoro Islands in the Indian Ocean and off Indonesia. They are endangered.

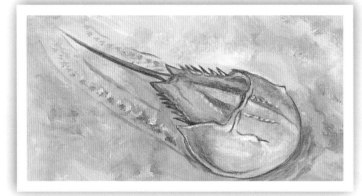

Horseshoe crabs (family Limulidae)

Horseshoe crabs are not crabs—they are more closely related to spiders and scorpions. They live on the east and southeast coasts of Asia, the Atlantic coast of North America, and in the Gulf of Mexico. They can be as small as a human hand or as large as a dinner plate. They can swim (upside down at an angle to the bottom of the ocean), but they crawl most of the time. Horseshoe crabs have copper in their blood, which makes the blood blue. A female horseshoe crab lays about 4,000 eggs at a time and between 60,000 and 120,000 eggs each year.

Dragonflies (order Odonata)

Insects take in oxygen through holes in their bodies called spiracles. When giant dragonfly relatives were alive 325 million to 250 million years ago, Earth's atmosphere contained up to 35 percent oxygen, much more than the 21 percent in the air today. Some scientists think that when oxygen levels fell at the end of the Paleozoic era (about 250 million years ago), large insects' bodies couldn't get enough oxygen. This may be one reason giant dragonfly relatives became extinct. The first true dragonflies appeared about 250 million years ago. Today, dragonflies live on every continent except Antarctica.

Tuatara (*Sphenodon punctatus*)

The tuatara gets its name from a Maori word meaning "peaks on back." After mating, a female tuatara lays up to nineteen soft-shelled eggs in her underground burrow. Each egg is about one inch long. The eggs develop slowly, hatching a year or more later. The temperature of the ground around the nest determines whether the eggs will develop into males (warmer soil) or females (cooler soil). Because female tuataras do not care for their eggs or young, newly hatched tuataras must fend for themselves. They grow to be twenty to thirty-one inches long.

Chambered Nautilus (*Nautilus pompilius*)

Nautiluses live in the tropical waters of the Pacific and Indian Oceans. A nautilus has a soft body, armlike tentacles, and a hard outer shell. As its body grows, the nautilus adds a new, larger chamber to its shell, closing off the previous one. By adjusting the amount of water and gas in each empty chamber, the nautilus can control how much it floats or sinks. The shell of an adult nautilus grows to about eight inches in diameter and may have more than thirty chambers.

Hula painted frog (*Latonia nigriventer*)

Hula painted frogs are so rare that little is known about them. They are about two inches long with wide-set eyes, long front limbs, and stubby snouts. Along with midwife toads and other painted frogs, Hula painted frogs are in a larger group known as disc-tongued frogs, for their short, round tongues. Unlike frogs that use their long tongues to catch prey, disc-tongued frogs catch food with their mouths.

Glossary

amphibian: cold-blooded vertebrate, such as a frog, toad, or newt, that spends part of its life in water and part on land

fossil: any part of an ancient plant or animal that is preserved in some way, or a preserved impression of a living organism

living fossil: informal term used to describe a plant or animal that has remained relatively unchanged over millions of years and typically has no close living relatives

mammal: warm-blooded animal with fur or hair; feeds its babies milk

mandible: the part of an insect's mouth that resembles a jaw and is often used for biting

Maori: indigenous, or native, people of New Zealand

molting: shedding old feathers, hair, or skin, or an old shell, to make way for new growth

peat: brown, soil-like material consisting of partly decomposed vegetable matter

reptiles: group of vertebrates that includes lizards, snakes, crocodiles, turtles, and dinosaurs

sediment: the sand and dirt that settles in the bottom of lakes

vertebrate: an animal with a backbone

For More Information

Books
Lawrence, Ellen. *A Dragonfly's Life*. New York: Bearport Publishing Company, 2013.

Pringle, Laurence. *Billions of Years, Amazing Changes: The Story of Evolution*. Honesdale, PA: Boyds Mills Press, 2011.

Walker, Sally M. *Fossil Fish Found Alive: Discovering the Coelacanth*. Minneapolis: Carolrhoda Books, 2002.

Websites
Aquarium of the Pacific, Long Beach, CA
http://www.aquariumofpacific.org/onlinelearningcenter/species/chambered_nautilus
Chambered nautilus facts and photo

BBC News
http://www.bbc.com/news/science-environment-22770959
An article about the 2011 discovery of the Hula painted frog

http://www.bbc.com/earth/story/20150413-can-an-animal-stop-evolving
An article about living fossils

International Wildlife Museum, Tucson, AZ
http://www.thewildlifemuseum.org/exhibits/Living-Fossils/
Easy-to-download PDFs about living-fossil species

Maryland Department of Natural Resources
http://dnr2.maryland.gov/fisheries/Pages/horseshoe-crab.aspx
Horseshoe crab facts and life history

San Diego Zoo, San Diego, CA
http://animals.sandiegozoo.org/animals/tuatara
In-depth facts and photos about tuataras